Masterpieces: Artists and Their Works

Rembrandt

by Xavier Niz

W

FRANKLIN WATTS
LONDON•SYDNEY

This edition first published in 2004 by

Franklin Watts
96 Leonard Street
London
EC2A 4XD

Franklin Watts Australia
45-51 Huntley Street
Alexandria
NSW 2015

ISBN 07496 5426 0

© Capstone Press. 2002, 2004
Series created by Bridgestone Books, published by Capstone Press 151 Good Counsel
Drive, P.O. Box 669, Mankato, Minnesota 56002

Printed in Hong Kong

Consultant: Joan Lingen, Ph.D. Professor of Art History, Clarke College, Iowa, USA

Cover Art: *Belshazzar's Feast* by Rembrandt van Rijn.

Editorial Credits

Editorial Credits
Blake Hoena, editor; Heather Kindseth, series designer; Juliette Peters, book designer;
    Alta Schaffer, photo researcher; Karen Risch, product planning editor

Photo Credits
Art Resource, 14; Mauritshuis, The Hague, Netherlands/Erich Lessing, 10; Scala, 12
Bridgeman Art Library/National Gallery, London, UK, cover (left) Mauritshuis,
    The Hague, Netherlands, cover (right); Isabella Stewart Gardner Museum,
    Boston, MA, USA, 4; Rijksmuseum, Amsterdam, Holland, 16
Corbis/National Gallery Collection; By kind permission of the Trustees of the National
    Gallery, London, 18
Museum of Fine Arts Boston, Zoe Oliver Sherman Collection given in memory of Lillie
    Oliver Poor, 24.8x31.7 cm, Rembrandt Harmensz van Rijn, Dutch 1606–1669, 8
SuperStock/Stadel Art Institute, Frankfurt am Main, 6; Rijksmuseum, Amsterdam,
    Holland, 20

Table of Contents

In *Storm on the Sea of Galilee*, Rembrandt used light to show the sailors' struggle against the storm's crashing waves.

Rembrandt van Rijn

Rembrandt van Rijn (1606–1669) was a famous Dutch painter. He often painted portraits and scenes from the Bible, such as *Belshazzar's Feast* (shown on the front cover). Rembrandt is famous for his use of shading. He used light and shadow to paint lifelike pictures and exciting scenes.

In the 1600s, artists made people look perfect in their **portraits**. Artists painted people with smooth skin and made them look better than they did in real life. But Rembrandt chose to paint what he saw. In his paintings, he used light and shadow to show peoples' wrinkles and blemishes.

Most artists painted people sitting still in portraits. Rembrandt liked to show action in his work. He painted doctors looking at a dead body. He painted soldiers getting ready for battle. Rembrandt wanted his paintings to be exciting.

In *The Blinding of Samson*, Samson's (bottom centre) toes and fists are curled in pain and anger. Rembrandt used body gestures to show what Samson is feeling as he is being attacked.

Young Rembrandt

Rembrandt was born in Leiden, Netherlands on 15th July 1606. As a boy, he was not interested in his school studies. He liked to draw. He often drew his family and the windmills near his home.

Rembrandt's father encouraged his son's talent. In around 1621, he sent Rembrandt to be **apprentice** to artist Jacob van Swanenburg. Swanenburg taught Rembrandt how to make paint and prepare **canvases**.

After three years, Swanenburg sent Rembrandt to study with Pieter Lastman. Lastman taught Rembrandt the importance of showing people's clothes and actions in art. Clothing could show if a person was rich or poor. Gestures could show if a person was happy, sad, or angry.

In 1625, when he was 19, Rembrandt opened an art studio in Leiden. He painted and sold scenes from the Bible. People also hired him to paint their portraits. He also painted self - portraits.

Light shines down on the painter's work in *Artist in His Studio*.
Rembrandt used light to show the importance of the painter's work.

Chiaroscuro

Rembrandt worked with light in his art. He would draw his father wearing fancy clothes and paint his mother doing chores. In these works, Rembrandt concentrated on the light shining on his parents. He used the light to show the details of their faces. Details helped show his parents' **expressions**.

While in Leiden, Rembrandt met a group of artists from Utrecht, Netherlands. These artists worked with a new art style called Chiaroscuro. **Chiaroscuro** used light and shadow to show dramatic scenes. Rembrandt worked with this style in paintings like *Artist in His Studio.*

Rembrandt's skills earned him respect as an artist. Wealthy people hired him to paint their portraits and art dealers from Amsterdam, bought his drawings.

In 1631, Rembrandt decided to move to Amsterdam. It was a large city where he could find plenty of work.

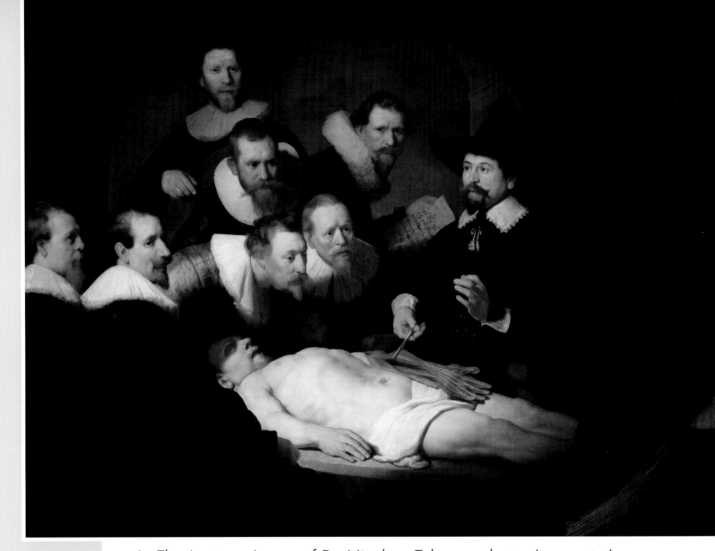

In *The Anatomy Lesson of Dr. Nicolaes Tulp*, one doctor (top centre) holds a piece of paper. The names of the eight doctors are written on the paper.

Anatomy Lessons

In Amsterdam, Dr. Nicolaes Tulp hired Rembrandt. Doctors asked artists to paint portraits of them and their students. Tulp wanted Rembrandt to paint a picture of him studying a dead body with seven other doctors.

Traditionally, artists lined up people in rows for portraits. But Rembrandt painted the doctors in a triangle shape. He then could show how they worked with each other.

Rembrandt painted light shining on the doctors' faces. The light shows detail such as lines and wrinkles. It also helps show the doctors' interest in Tulp's work.

The Anatomy Lesson of Dr. Nicolaes Tulp made Rembrandt a popular portrait painter. Tulp and his colleagues were happy with his work. Other doctors hired Rembrandt to make similar paintings.

In *Saskia as Flora*, Rembrandt had his wife wear fine clothes. He liked to show off his wealth by having Saskia wear expensive clothes and jewellery in her portraits.

Amsterdam

In 1634, Rembrandt married Saskia van Uglenburgh. She was the niece of his art dealer, Hendrick van Uglenburgh.

In the 1630s, Rembrandt was busy with work. Many people wanted him to paint their portraits. He earned a great deal of money selling his paintings, but he quickly spent the money. Rembrandt bought fine clothes, artwork and expensive jewellery.

During this time, Rembrandt had several students helping him. Apprentices mixed paints and sometimes drew the outlines of portraits. Rembrandt then filled in the details of the paintings. With his students' help, Rembrandt could work on several paintings at one time.

When Rembrandt was not working, he looked for new ideas. Amsterdam was a large city. People from all over the world lived there. Rembrandt enjoyed drawing these people and the different clothes they wore. He also visited the countryside and drew **landscapes**. Rembrandt used many of his **sketches** to create new works of art.

In *The Little Children Being Brought to Jesus,* parents bring their children to Jesus (centre) to be blessed. In this print, light shines from Jesus, brightening the centre of the picture.

Etchings

During his life, Rembrandt created many etchings. **Etchings** are pictures made on a metal plate. The plate is then covered with ink and used to make prints of the picture. Etchings allow artists to make many copies of a drawing quickly.

Before Rembrandt, artists used hatching in etchings. **Hatching** is a series of parallel lines. Artists shaded a picture with hatching. Rembrandt thought hatching limited the amount of detail he could show. Instead, he used his etching tool like a pencil. He drew lines of different thickness to shade and add detail to his work.

Rembrandt's etchings gained him even more fame. Rich people in Amsterdam bought copies of his prints.

In 1641, Rembrandt's son, Titus, was born. Soon after this, Saskia became ill and died. Saddened, Rembrandt spent most of his time working on paintings and etchings.

In the centre of *The Night Watch*, Captain Cocq talks to one of his
soldiers. A light shines on them, showing that they are important.
The other soldiers are in shadow.

The Night Watch

In 1642, Captain Frans Banning Cocq hired Rembrandt. to paint a life-sized painting of him and his soldiers. Rembrandt worked on this painting day and night for a year. It showed the soldiers in action. They look as if they might be getting ready for battle. Rembrandt thought the painting would look lifelike if the soldiers appeared to be doing something.

Cocq was pleased with the painting, but many of his soldiers were not. They wanted a more traditional portrait. These soldiers were upset that they were not easily seen in the painting. Some of them are standing behind other soldiers. Some soldiers are not completely in the painting.

Today, *The Shooting Company of Captain Frans Banning Cocq* is known as *The Night Watch.* It had become blackened with tobacco smoke over the years. The smoke made people think the painting was of a night scene.

Rembrandt painted *Hendrickje Bathing in a River* in 1655. Many of his later works were self-portraits and paintings of his family.

Later Years

In 1649, Rembrandt hired a nurse, Hendrickje Stoffels. She took care of Titus. Rembrandt fell in love with Hendrickje. In 1654, they had a daughter, Cornelia.

In his later years, Rembrandt did not earn enough money to support his family. Few people bought his paintings. He also owed a great deal of money. He had bought many fine clothes, a large house, and a great deal of artwork.

In 1656, Rembrandt sold many of his belongings to pay his debts. He also sold his house. Rembrandt then moved his family to a small house in a poor part of Amsterdam.

In 1660, Titus and Hendrickje opened a small art shop. They sold Rembrandt's work to earn money to support the family.

Rembrandt's last years were sad ones. He was poor. In 1663, Hendrickje died and five years later, Titus died. On 4th October, 1669, Rembrandt died. He was 63.

In *The Syndics of the Clothmakers' Guild,* the men look like they were interrupted during an important meeting. Rembrandt is famous for painting scenes that give a feeling of action.

Rembrandt's Fame

Rembrandt earned great success during his life. He sold many works of art and never stopped working. He created more than 600 paintings, 300 etchings, and 1,400 drawings.

Rembrandt's work influenced many artists. His style of etching changed the way prints were made. Artists study his use of light and shadow to learn how to make paintings lifelike.

Today, Rembrandt's artwork is in museums around the world. The National Gallery in London and The Louvre Museum in Paris show his work, The Metropolitan Museum of Art in New York has a large collection of his art. The most important collection of Rembrandt's art is at the Rijksmuseum in Amsterdam.

Timeline

1606 - Rembrandt is born in Leiden, Netherlands on 15th July

1621 - Jacob Swanenburg makes Rembrandt his apprentice.

1624 - Rembrandt goes to Amsterdam to study
with Pieter Lastman.

1625 - Rembrandt opens an art studio in Leiden.

1629 - Rembrandt paints *Artist in His Studio*.

1631 - Rembrandt moves to Amsterdam.

1632 - Rembrandt paints *The Anatomy Lesson of Dr. Nicolaes Tulp*.

1634 - Rembrandt marries Saskia van Uglenburgh; he paints
Saskia as Flora.

1641 - Rembrandt's son, Titus, is born.

1642 - Saskia dies; Rembrandt paints *The Night Watch*.

1649 - Hendrickje Stoffels becomes Titus' nurse.

1654 - Rembrandt's daughter, Cornelia, is born.

1656 - Rembrandt sells his house and many of his belongings to
pay his debts.

1662 - Rembrandt paints *The Syndics of the Clothmakers' Guild*.

1669 - Rembrandt dies on 4th October Amsterdam.

Useful Websites

www.nationalgallery.org.uk/
This is the official site for The
National Gallery. It is easy to
navigate and provides you
with everything you need to
know about the collection as
well as biographies and
pictures to download. It also
provides help with the
biblical stories that
Rembrandt used for
inspiration.

www.rijksmuseum.nl/asp/st
art..asp?language=uk
Another official site, this time
for The Rijksmuseum in
Amsterdam. The information
here is comprehensive and
provides neat explanations
for the pictures as well as
images and biography.

www.ibiblio.org/wm/paint/
auth/vinci
This site offers biographical
detail as well as lots of
fascinating information about
the paintings themselves.

Note to parents and teachers
Every effort has been made by the
Publishers to ensure that
these websites are suitable for
children; that they are of the
highest educational value, and
that they contain no
inappropriate or offensive
material. However, because of the
nature of the Internet, it is
impossible to guarantee that the
contents of these sites will not be
altered.We strongly advise that
Internet access is supervised by a
responsible adult.

Glossary

anatomy - the study of the human body

apprentice - someone who learns a trade or craft by working with a skilled person

canvas - a cloth surface for painting

Chiaroscuro - an art style using light and shadow to create a dramatic scene

etching - a picture created on a metal plate; artists use etchings to make prints of pictures

hatchings - a series of parallel lines used in etchings

expression - the act of showing feelings

landscape - a painting or drawing of an outdoor scene

portrait - a drawing or painting of a person

sketch - a rough drawing

Index